Fnl
publications

Once on a warm sunny day.....

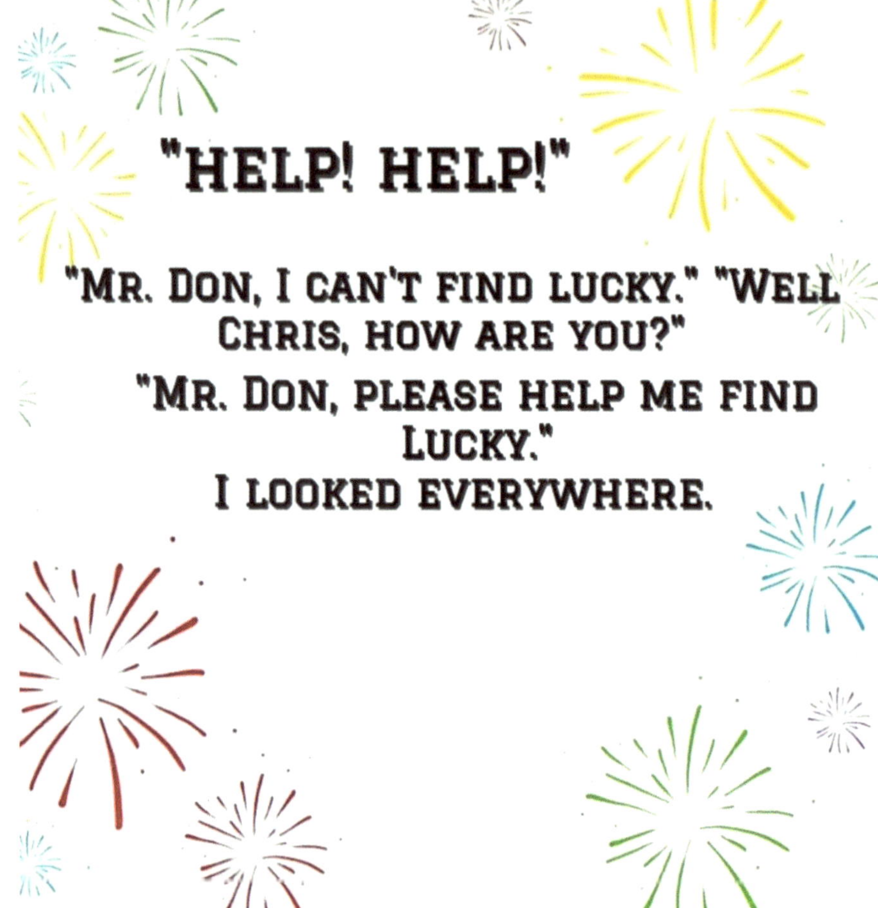

"HELP! HELP!"

"MR. DON, I CAN'T FIND LUCKY." "WELL CHRIS, HOW ARE YOU?"
"MR. DON, PLEASE HELP ME FIND LUCKY."
I LOOKED EVERYWHERE.

Mr. Don happily
said yes.
"Ok Chris, where did you last
see him?"

"I let him out to play, but when
I came back he was gone,"
yells Chris.

"Lucky!"

CAN YOU HELP ME FIND Lucky?

So Mr.Don and Chris went looking for Lucky.

They asked the mailman,

"No, sorry Chris."

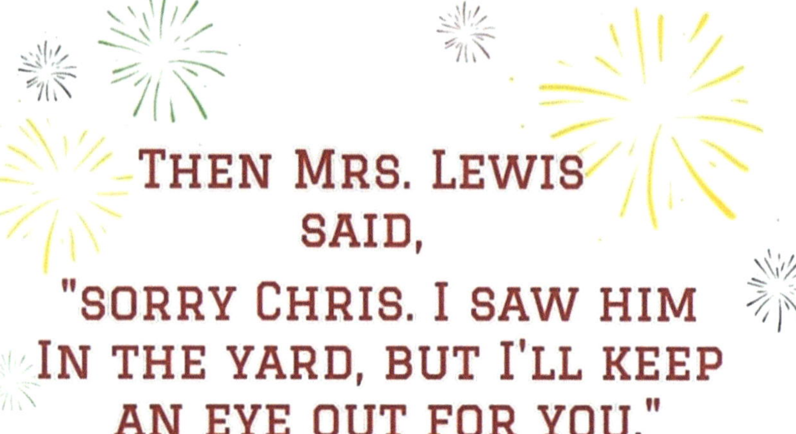

THEN MRS. LEWIS
SAID,

"SORRY CHRIS. I SAW HIM
IN THE YARD, BUT I'LL KEEP
AN EYE OUT FOR YOU."

THE PARK
WAS EMPTY TOO AND CHRIS WAS STARTING TO GET WORRIED.

OH NO!

"HEY, CHRIS. KEEP LOOKING. I'M SURE HE WILL SHOW UP." MR. DON WENT HOME TO EAT DINNER.

"Bye Chris."

BUT CHRIS DIDN'T KNOW
WHERE TO LOOK. HE
CHECKED EVERYWHERE
LUCKY COULD
BE...........

"Oh,
no!"

Do you see Lucky?

CHRIS THOUGHT ABOUT
HIS TREE HOUSE.
MAYBE HE COULD SEE
HIS LITTLE FRIEND
FROM ABOVE.

What a surprise!

He found lucky playing with his favorite ball in the tree house.

Hooray!

EXCITED,
WITH JOY,
CHRIS TOOK HIS
PAL DOWN THE SLIDE AS
THEY BOTH WENT HOME.

THE END.

T&P Thomas would like
to thank friends,family
and all involved for
making this book a
success.
Peace and love.